SUMMARY OF

HOW TO RAISE

SUCCESSFUL PEOPLE:

Simple Lessons for Radical Results |

Esther Wojcicki

Cityprint

NOTE: This is a summary guide and is meant as a companion to, not a replacement for, the original book.

Our summaries are designed to teach you important lessons in a cost-effective and timely manner. They are coherent, concise and complete, highlighting the main ideas and concepts contained in the original books. Non-essential information is removed to save the reader hours of reading time. Save time and money by completing your reading list.

PLEASE FOLLOW THIS LINK TO GET REGULAR NEW BOOK SUMMARY GUIDES:

https://amazon.com/author/cityprint

ABOUT BOOK:

How to Raise Successful People (2019) explores the secrets of great parenting. Drawing on a lifetime of experience in getting the best out of young people, educator and mother Esther Wojcicki examines how you can raise your children to be not only successful, but kind and independent too.

ABOUT THE AUTHOR;

Esther Wojcicki is a journalist, educator and the mother of two of Silicon Valley's most successful female entrepreneurs, Susan and Anne Wojcicki. The creator of the Palo Alto High School Media Arts Program in California, Wojcicki's pedagogical approaches have been adopted by schools around the world.

In 2002, she was named California Teacher of the Year.

INTRODUCTION.

Be the parent your child needs.

In the 1960s, when journalist and educator Esther Wojcicki was a new, young mother, she struggled to know where to turn for parenting advice. Nowadays, things have changed. In fact, modern parents are bombarded with tips and strategies on how to raise their children right. Unfortunately, though, much of this advice focuses on how to help your child become a high achiever, often through micromanaging their actions, rather than how to develop a happy, well-adjusted member of society.

That's where Esther Wojcicki comes in. Instead of focusing purely on success and achievement, her advice highlights the unsung values you should be passing on to your children, like trust, respect and independence. Drawing on the poignant real-life experiences of her own family, as well as those of her students, these summary show you how you can excel at the most important job you'll ever have: raising the next generation.

Read on to discover

- What you can learn from your own childhood;
- How much structure your child really needs; and
- Why parents shouldn't behave like helicopters.

BECOMING A BETTER PARENT REQUIRES TAKING THE BEST OF YOUR PARENTS' EFFORTS AND LEAVING THE REST.

When it comes to parenting, it's a known fact that we tend to raise our children in the same way our parents raised us. Now, this might not sound so bad if you enjoyed a happy and contented childhood. But the reality is that many of us have experienced some sort of childhood trauma, or had parents who made serious mistakes.

Growing up in an orthodox Jewish family in the 1950s, the author experienced her fair share of damaging parental behavior. At the tender age of five, her father told her that boys were more important than girls, and her upbringing reflected this attitude. While her younger brother Lee was showered with attention, toys and extra helpings at dinner, she watched from the sidelines, rarely given anything to play with. Sometimes she was even scolded for eating too much at mealtimes. Her parents' religion informed their belief that a woman's place was in the home, and at age eighteen, when she rejected marriage in favor of attending college, her parents cut her off financially.

In spite of her difficult beginnings – or perhaps because of them – the author was determined to raise her own children in a spirit of support and acceptance. As part of this process, she took the time to reevaluate her own childhood experiences. By reassessing them with the benefit of an adult perspective, she thought, she could choose which parenting behaviors she wanted to emulate and which she really didn't.

Her father's example, that of a distant and authoritarian figure, was something that she definitely wanted to avoid. Her mother, on the other hand, had been consistently warm and loving; the author has tried to replicate this and build an equally close relationship with her own daughters while rejecting the unyielding sexism expressed by her father.

In an effort to avoid her father's mistakes, she constantly taught her daughters to exert control over their own lives by making choices. She developed their decision-making abilities by asking them questions like, "Is it a banana or an orange that you want?" or "Do you want to paint a picture or play in the yard?" Questions like these might seem insignificant, but for the author, they represented an important break with the suffocating sexism of her own childhood.

In the next summary, you'll discover one parenting habit you should definitely pass on to the next generation – the ability to trust.

THERE'S A DEFICIT OF TRUST IN THE MODERN WORLD, BUT IT'S IMPORTANT THAT PARENTS HAVE FAITH IN THEIR CHILDREN.

In her new role as a grandparent, the author often looks after her grandchildren while her own daughter Susan is at work. One morning, the author dropped her eight-year-old granddaughters off at a Target store, allowing them to shop on their own for an hour. Watching them skip into the shop, she felt a surge of pride in their newfound independence. However, when their mother Susan found out about the trip, she saw things very differently.

Susan was not impressed. "Anything could have happened to them!" she protested. Of course, nothing did happen, and the girls were picked up safe and sound.

Unfortunately, though, Susan's overblown fear that something bad would happen to her daughters reflects the breakdown of trust in wider American society.

The 2018 Edelman Trust Barometer, a survey of how much the general population trusts its country's institutions, found that the United States had fallen by nine points on the Global Trust Scale – the biggest drop in trust ever recorded.

And it's not just our institutions. Depressingly, Americans no longer trust their neighbors, either.

A 2015 Pew Research study found that only 52 percent of people in the United States agree that they can trust their neighbors. And most shockingly of all, just 19 percent of American millennials believe that most people are trustworthy.

Looking at these damning statistics, it's no wonder that Susan didn't trust that her children would be safe alone that day. Unfortunately, though, by preventing our children from doing things independently, we are not only teaching them that the world cannot be trusted – we are also teaching our children that they themselves cannot be trusted.

This is an issue. It's crucial for children's self-esteem that they feel as if their parents believe in their abilities and trust them to do things. If you give your children the impression that they can't be trusted to visit a Target store by themselves, or play in the street without adult supervision, then this message gets internalized. The result? Your child will consider herself to be untrustworthy, and she'll express this belief by behaving in an untrustworthy way. Research shows that untrustworthy children are less likely to engage in sharing and collaborative behavior, and are more likely to exhibit aggression.

With negative effects like these, it's clearly worth it to make your children feel trusted by permitting them to do things on their own once in a while!

FAILING TO RESPECT YOUR CHILD'S CHOICES CAN HAVE DAMAGING AND EVEN DEADLY CONSEQUENCES.

When the author's daughter Anne graduated from college, she surprised everyone by announcing that she had no intention of pursuing a professional career at all; instead, she wanted to live at home and work as a babysitter.

While many parents would have panicked at this lack of ambition, the author's attitude was much more relaxed. This was Anne's life, she figured, and she would find her own way in her own time. Unfortunately, during her career as a teacher, the author has seen many parents take a much stronger stance against their children's life choices, often with detrimental outcomes.

Her former student Greg, for example, was a talented high school student with a passion for graphic design.

His parents, though, were dead set on him becoming a scientist. Why? They themselves were scientists and were narrow-minded about other career paths. When Greg showed little interest in science at school, they pressured him into taking extra classes, which gave him less and less time for his beloved art. The result? Greg became increasingly withdrawn and depressed as time went on.

Thankfully, Greg managed to wade through the misery and parental pressure of his younger years, and today he's a successful graphic artist with the life that he – not his parents – wanted. But not all teenagers with interfering parents come out on the other side. When parents fail to respect their children's choices, it can lead to a family's total devastation.

Researchers at Yale University have discovered that, among adolescents from affluent American communities,

feeling isolated from one's parents
is a major cause of suicide. In the
author's experience, such isolation
typically starts with parents' lack
of respect for their children's
preferences, which leads to teenagers
resenting or fearing their parents.
The parent-child relationship then
deteriorates further, often leading
to a complete communication
breakdown.

Of course, the topic of teen suicide
is a complex one, and many factors
can increase the risk of suicide.
Nevertheless, at the heart of this
disturbing phenomenon is a teenager's
feeling of being trapped and having
to live a life she didn't choose for
herself. When this feeling becomes
overwhelming, young people sometimes
choose to take the only way out they
see open to them.

Letting your children choose their
own paths by respecting their life
choices can prevent this from

happening. The author's daughter, for
example, eventually got a great job
with an investment firm after her
spell of babysitting – no parental
pressure required.

SUCCESSFUL CHILDREN HAVE TRUE GRIT AND A HEALTHY ATTITUDE TOWARD FAILURE .

Getting what we want can take a while. The author has seen many of her students learn this the hard way. One of them, Gady, was a talented writer and extremely helpful to the other students he worked with on the high school newspaper. Unfortunately, Gady's classmates failed to recognize his merits, and selected someone else to act as the newspaper's editor-in-chief.

But was Gady crushed by his classmates' snub? Far from it. He picked himself up and continued writing the best articles he could for the newspaper, all the while helping others with their pieces, too. When the time came, Gady applied to Harvard University. He didn't have the grades the prestigious college usually required, but Harvard was so impressed by his great attitude that they offered him a place anway. These days, Gady is the Media Editor for the Economist, one of the world's most prestigious magazines.

The author believes that many children and parents today can learn a valuable lesson from Gady's chequered path to success: the importance of having grit.

Grit means sticking with your goals, even in the face of tough obstacles and adversity. In her 2014 book Grit: The Power of Passion and Perseverance, psychologist Angela Duckworth examined the lives of extremely successful people. She discovered that these individuals all had two things in common. One was crystal-clear goals. The other was a ferocious drive to achieve these goals, marked by uncommonly high levels of resilience and an unusually strong work ethic. In other words, they had a lot of grit.

You can instill grit in your children by equipping them with a growth outlook on life.

In her 2006 book Mindset, psychologist Carol Dweck outlines two possible attitudes toward achievement. The first is a fixed outlook – believing that one's abilities are innate and unchangeable. But those with a growth outlook believe that hard work and determination are responsible for success, not innate ability. They believe that failing at something is not a reason to give up, and as a result, they simply have more grit.

Nurture a growth outlook in your children by rewarding them for commitment and effort, rather than for simply being "great" at something. And conversely, try not to give them the impression that failure means they're not smart. After all, if Gady had taken his high school newspaper failure as a measure of his abilities, he might never have pursued his dream.

AN AUTHORITATIVE PARENTING STYLE IS GOOD, BUT A COLLABORATIVE STYLE MAY BE EVEN BETTER.

Modern parenting advice often tells parents they need to set boundaries for their children, such as dictating when they must go to bed, or how much they need to eat at the dinner table. A failure to be firm, it seems, will result in the little people running the show. But does more parental control really make for better parenting?

The complex truth is that some structure is good for children, but their mental health can suffer when too much is placed on them.

This was highlighted in a 1971 study by developmental psychologist Diana Baumrind that looked at families with children of preschool age. The researchers identified significant differences between an authoritative parenting style and an authoritarian one.

While an authoritarian style emphasized parental inflexibility and a demand for constant obedience, an authoritative parenting style, while still firm, was also characterized by positivity and a willingness to discuss things with the child. This distinction is important, because researchers found that an authoritative but not an authoritarian style led to independent, focused behavior among the preschoolers, as well as a greater sense of responsibility toward others. Furthermore, Baumrind's follow-up study in 1991 found that those children who had experienced authoritative parenting were less likely to become involved with drugs during adolescence.

However, the author believes there may be an even better parenting style that psychologists have yet to explore. She calls it collaborative parenting.

In this style, the parent works with the child to get things done, rather than simply telling her what to do. For instance, whereas an authoritarian parent might pick out a color for their child's bedroom and then instruct the child on how to paint the room, a collaborative parent makes a decision about the color with their child, and then proceeds to pick out the right paint brushes with them, too. Thus, the child has a degree of agency over the task at hand, and feels like a collaborator rather than just a worker.

It's never too early to start collaborative parenting. One study found that, even at three years old, children understood the concept of working in partnership with someone else, and were able to appreciate others' viewpoints along with their own.

Good parents aren't afraid to set boundaries, but, equally, great parents aren't afraid to treat their child as a trusted collaborator once in a while.

CHILDREN AND THEIR PARENTS NOW PRIORITIZE PERSONAL ACHIEVEMENT OVER KINDNESS.

When the author's terminally ill mother moved into a hospice, her family hoped the dying woman would receive the care and support she needed. But shockingly, she was ignored and neglected by hospice staff. This was where the author's daughter Anne stepped in. Driven by love and compassion, Anne took two weeks off work to find a better facility for her grandmother, where she would be well-treated during whatever time she had left.

This family crisis demonstrates both how kind and unkind humanity can be. At our worst, we are the indifferent hospice staff; at our best, we are Anne and her heartfelt commitment to her grandmother. Worryingly, though, evidence suggests there aren't many Annes among the younger generation.

This sad state of affairs is illustrated by Harvard University's Making Caring Common Project, a research initiative that examined the attitudes of 10,000 children toward compassionate behavior. Depressingly, researchers found that 80 percent of these children identified their own personal happiness or success as their main priority in life, with only 20 percent selecting "caring for others" as their top goal.

Moreover, the researchers discovered that the majority of children surveyed felt that their parents would be prouder of them for doing well academically than for caring about others in the community.

So what's behind this collapse in kindness among American young people? Unfortunately, the answer may lie in the damaging parenting style known as helicopter parenting.

So called for their tendency to "hover" around their children, helicopter parents are preoccupied with doing everything possible to maximize their children's chances of success. From driving them to endless extracurricular activities to scrutinizing their report cards minutely, helicopter parents care only about whether their child will win, and not at all about whether their child is kind.

The author saw this cut-throat attitude up close, at a talk by author Amy Chua. Chua is a second-generation Chinese-American who expounds the virtues of achievement-driven parenting in her book Battle Hymn of the Tiger Mother. Chua's sentiments on that day? She said she never even considered whether her family was a kind or a happy one – she only cared that her children bested the competition in everything they did. And Chua is an enormously popular figure; her book a best seller!

GRATITUDE IS INVALUABLE, AND IT CAN BE TAUGHT.

Helping your child develop into a kind person has obvious advantages for the people around him. After all, who wouldn't want to live next door to someone who's always willing to do you a favor, or who cares about your well-being?

But what about the benefits for kind people themselves? In other words, does it benefit your child to be kind?

The evidence says that it does. Take gratitude, for instance, an important element of kindness. Showing gratitude means recognizing all the ways in which others improve our lives and demonstrating our appreciation for them. And studies have found that showing gratitude has clear benefits for our mental health.

For instance, a 2018 study published in the Journal of Positive Psychology found that a grateful outlook boosted people's happiness levels, and increased the amount of hope they had for the future. Furthermore, the Journal of School Psychology has published research revealing that adolescents with a grateful mindset have higher levels of optimism, a greater feeling of life satisfaction and a lower risk of depression.

So how can you give your child the invaluable gift of gratitude?

Well, your children are often your keenest observers, so start by setting an example with your own behavior. Christmas provides the perfect opportunity to do this. As you gather 'round the Christmas tree, don't be one of those families that tears through gifts as if it's a race, without anyone ever stopping to say "thank you" for anything. Instead, show your children that every gift should be lingered over, even if it's something they didn't

ask for or particularly want.
Encourage them to take time with the
process of unwrapping, so that they
can reflect on the money and time
someone spent getting that present
for them.

You can also cultivate gratitude in
your children by encouraging them to
keep a diary of all the things
they're grateful for. Studies have
shown that writing down what we're
thankful for actually stimulates our
brains to feel even more grateful.
The author looks back fondly on the
travel diaries her daughters kept as
children, and believes the diaries
helped them have a greater
appreciation for what they were
experiencing each day.

Gratitude is like kindness,
independence and a collaborative
spirit: by giving our children these
gifts, along with our trust and
respect, we can truly change the
world.

FINAL SUMMARY.

The key message in these summary:

All too often, modern parents hover around their children, stage-managing their paths to success and denying them a valuable taste of independence. So instead of treating your children like your shadow, try showing them trust, respect and kindness by letting them find their own way.

Actionable advice:

Model the behavior you want to teach.

As parents, the attitudes we display are the ones our children will adopt as well. Over her teaching career, the author has often seen this firsthand. As she learned, if a child is unreasonably distraught by an academic setback, chances are he learned that behavior from a parent. So if you want your child to develop into a resilient individual who copes well with failure, why not try modeling a positive outlook yourself? If your child has a setback in school, take it in stride and focus on what can be done to fix the problem. After all, our children do as we do, not as we say.

Made in the USA
San Bernardino, CA
16 May 2019